MADE IN ENGLAND THE BEST OF JULIAN LLOYD WEBBER

EDITED BY JULIAN LLOYD WEBBER

The pieces in this collection have been selected by Julian Lloyd Webber from his acclaimed CD
MADE IN ENGLAND
Catalogue number 476118-6
(Universal Classics)

This publication is not authorised for sale in Europe

PIANO SCORE

WISE PUBLICATIONS
part of The Music Sales Group
London/New York/Paris/Sydney/Copenhagen/Berlin/Madrid/Tokyo

13-95

Exclusive distributors:
Music Sales Limited
8/9 Frith Street, London W1D 3JB, England.
Music Sales Pty Limited
120 Rothschild Avenue, Rosebery, NSW 2018, Australia.

Order No. AM976679
ISBN 0-7119-9851-5

Music engraved by Camden Music.

Your Guarantee of Quality:

As publishers, we strive to produce every book
to the highest commercial standards.

The book has been carefully designed to
minimise awkward page turns and to make
playing from it a real pleasure.

Particular care has been given to specifying
acid-free, neutral-sized paper made from pulps which
have not been elemental chlorine bleached.

This pulp is from farmed sustainable forests and
was produced with special regard for the environment.

Throughout, the printing and binding have been
planned to ensure a sturdy, attractive publication
which should give years of enjoyment.

If your copy fails to meet our high standards,
please inform us and we will gladly replace it.

Printed in the United Kingdom by
Caligraving Limited, Thetford, Norfolk.

www.musicsales.com

MADE IN ENGLAND is a collection of pieces chosen from the recordings I have made over a period of more than twenty years for Universal Classics.

They mix old favourites (like *The Swan* and *Kol Nidrei*) with more recent compositions like my own *Jackie's Song* and *Song For Baba* and Elton John's *Your Song*. None of the pieces are especially difficult - but, then, everything is difficult to play well!

I hope you enjoy this collection.

Julian Lloyd Webber

Julian Lloyd Webber

ADAGIO

composed by Tomaso Albinoni & Remo Giazotto
arranged by Julian Lloyd Webber

Cadenza
II

Con. Ped. sempre staccato

49
f
53
ff
57
ff
61
II I
II I

65
69
74
78
dim.
dim.
ad lib.
f
ff
p

BERCEUSE

FROM 'DOLLY SUITE'

composed by Gabriel Fauré

arranged by Julian Lloyd Webber

16
II
II
p
p sempre
21
26
II
31
sub. p

35
mp
sempre dolce
40
II
44
II
48

52
II
56
II
II
pp
pp
60
II
64
mp

68
72
76
80
p
II

AIR ON A G STRING

composed by Johann Sebastian Bach
arranged by Julian Lloyd Webber

11
13
cresc. poco a poco
cresc. poco a poco
15
18
poco rit.
poco rit.

AVE MARIA

composed by Giulio Romano Caccini
arranged by Julian Lloyd Webber

21
26
30
f
34
II
I

38
42
46
f
50
II

54
f
58
II
I
63
pp
pp
68
II
I
rall.
rall.

JACKIE'S SONG

composed by Julian Lloyd Webber
arranged by Julian Lloyd Webber & Pamela Chowhan

A
3
mp
B
Poco agitato
mf

senza ped.
RH
LH
RH
LH
C
Tempo primo (poco largamente)

D
molto dim.
f
mf
p
molto rall.
p
pp
mp molto espressivo

JESU, JOY OF MAN'S DESIRING

composed by Johann Sebastian Bach
arranged by Julian Lloyd Webber

11
14
p
17
mf
20

23
II
mf
p
27
mf
p
30
mf
33

36
39
mf
p
42
mf
45
I
p

48
51
54
57
mf
p

60
mf
63
mf
p
66
I
69
rit.
III

KOL NIDREI

composed by Max Bruch
arranged by Julian Lloyd Webber

Adagio ma non troppo

16
cresc.
pp
cresc.
p
19
dolce
5
pp legato
rfz
mf
22
p
p
ten.
p
26
cresc.
f
ten.
ten.
ten.
cresc.
pp

B
p
ff
p
cresc.
ff
p
p
cresc.
f
cresc.
C
con brio
fz
fp
dolce

42
rfz
p
p dolce
44
fp
47
D
espress.
cresc.
f
tremolo
ten.
cresc.
50
rfz
f
L.H.
trem.

52
f
p
pp
55
p dim.
ten.
pp
sempre
E
59
Un poco più animato
ten.
ten.
Ped.
61
Ped.

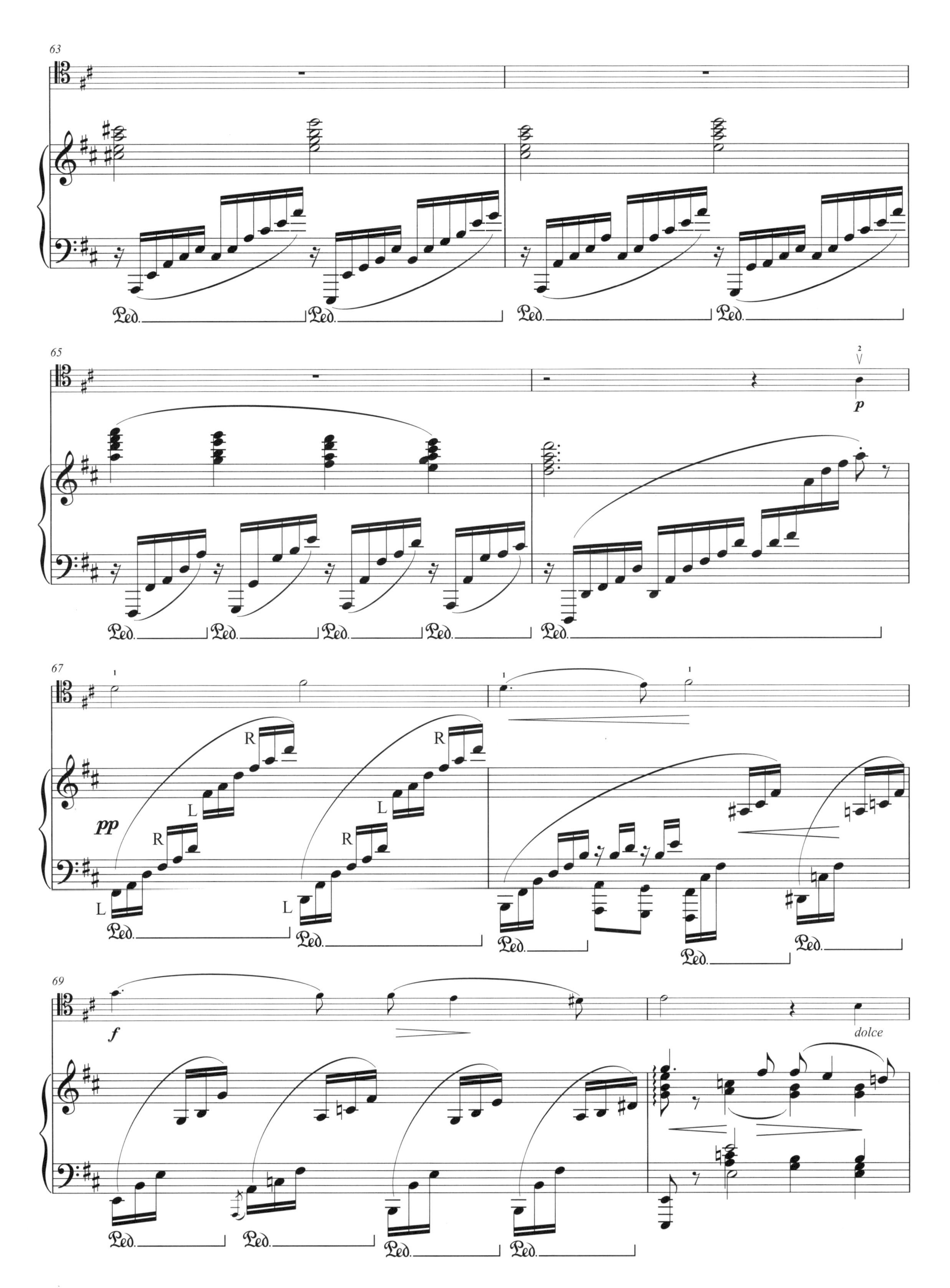
63
Ped.
65
p
Ped.
67
pp
R
L
Ped.
69
f
dolce
Ped.

71
cresc.
R
L
R
sim.
L
Ped.
Ped.
Ped.
73
F
f
p
75
f
(p)
Ped.
Ped.
77
f
p
Ped.
Ped.

79
f
mf
p
Ped.
Ped.
81
dolce
83
pp
f
85

87
ppp
cresc.
rit.
G
A tempo
89
pp
pp legato
92
poco
p
cresc.
95
pp
ten.

99
ten.
pp
ten.
Ped.
102
H
p
105
pp
109
I
tranquillo
morendo
ppp

MEDITATION

FROM 'THAÏS'

composed by Jules Massenet
arranged by Julian Lloyd Webber

rall.
a tempo
espressivo
cresc.
Poco più mosso
più f
poco più apass.
très expressif

34
più mosso agitato
sfz
più f
f
38
poco rit.
rall.
a tempo
p
dim.
II
pp
ff
43
rall.
p
f
48
a tempo
più f
cresc.

espressivo
cresc.
rall.
a tempo
rall.
a tempo
cresc.
calmato

SHEPHERD'S LULLABY

composed by T. J. Hewitt
arranged by Pamela Chowhan

11
15
II
II
19
23

27
pp
pp
31
I
35
f
f
39
II

43
ppp
ppp
Ped.
Ped.
Ped.
47
II
Ped.
Ped.
51
54

SONG FOR BABA

composed by Julian Lloyd Webber

P
pp
una corda
mp
8va
Ped.
una corda

SONGS MY MOTHER TAUGHT ME

composed by Antonín Dvořák
arranged by Julian Lloyd Webber

13

17
f
dim.

21
p

25
pp

30
1
2
II
4

34
1
2
II

38
3
f
cresc.
f

42
dim.
II
pp
dim.
pp

46
2
2
morendo
morendo

THE SWAN

FROM 'CARNIVAL OF THE ANIMALS'

composed by Camille Charles Saint-Saëns
arranged by Julian Lloyd Webber

* Although often marked 'Adagio' in arrangements, this is the marking in the full score.

8
9
11
13

15
17
p
pp
19
21
mf

23
2
dim.
dim.

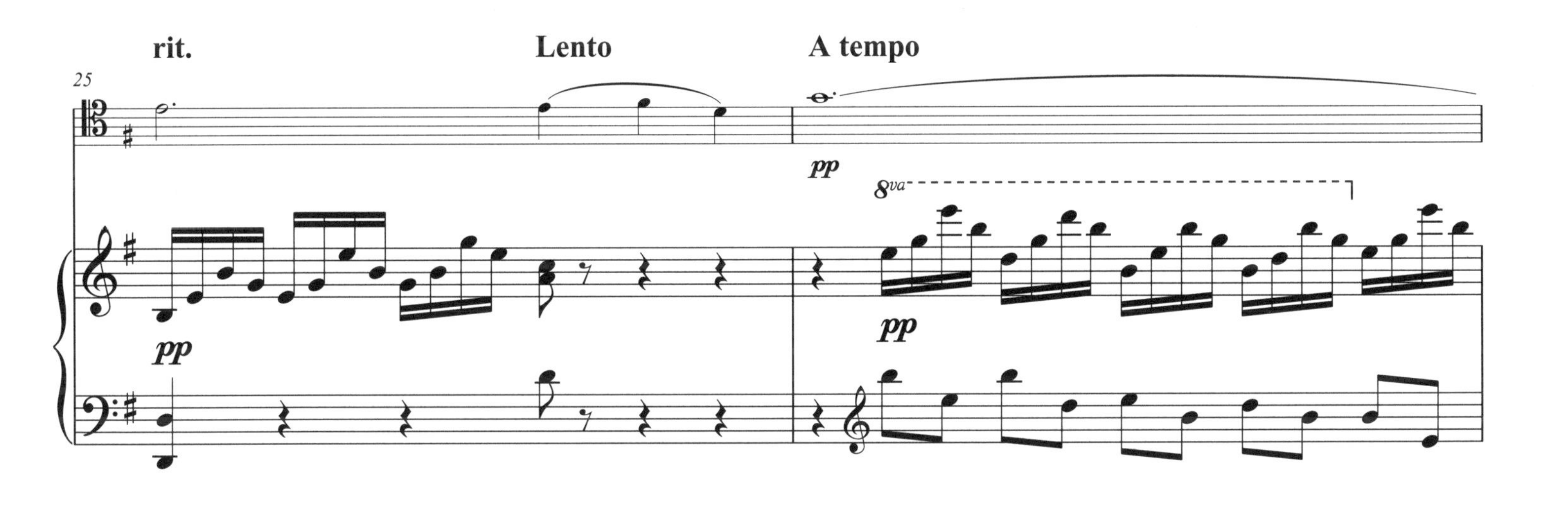
rit.
Lento
A tempo
25
pp
8va
pp
pp

rit.
27

YOUR SONG

words & music by Elton John & Bernie Taupin
arranged by Julian Lloyd Webber

7

9
1.
I

12
2.

15
17
to Coda
19
dolce
rit.
21
A tempo
D.S. al Coda (without repeat)

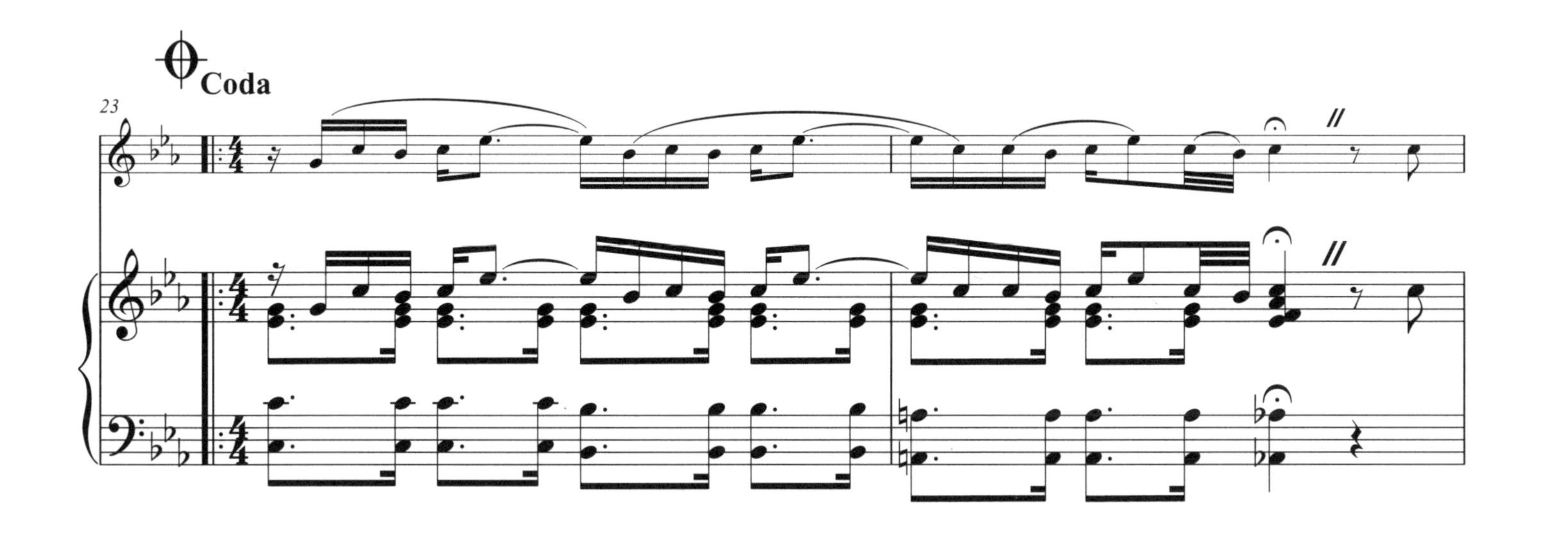
Coda
23

rit.
25
1.
A tempo

28
2.
A tempo
3
II